WHAT TO DO WITH THE GIFTED CHILD

Meeting The Needs Of The Gifted Child
In The Regular Classroom

by Judith Cochran

Incentive Publications, Inc.
Nashville, Tennessee

Cover by Susan Harrison
Edited by Jan Keeling

Library of Congress Catalog Card Number: 92-71469
ISBN 0-86530-174-3

TABLE OF CONTENTS

OVERVIEW/ IDENTIFICATION

Addressing the needs of gifted students has been a problem plaguing educators for decades. Gifted children are a precious natural resource that must be nurtured with the utmost care. Properly identifying and challenging them is a task to be taken seriously.

The politics of district funding for gifted programs rarely promises the long-term commitment these children sorely need. Realistically, the majority of gifted children will remain in regular classrooms because:

1. Funding and personnel aren't available for specialized gifted programs.
2. The gifted student is simply not identified.

As a result, there is a pressing need to accommodate gifted students in the regular classroom. This can be done by offering 1) a modified independent study program within the regular classroom, and 2) an expedient way to identify the students who could benefit from such a program.

In the past, the term "gifted" described people with high scores on I.Q. tests. Now, new concepts have expanded the definition of intelligence to include other dimensions. Joseph Renzulli's definition of gifted behavior will be the one accepted and adhered to in this handbook. Renzulli maintains that gifted children generally possess a cluster of three traits:

1. They have above average intelligence.
2. They are self-motivated and committed to task.
3. They are creative.

It is essential that the students identified as gifted exhibit a high level of self-motivation and commitment to task since they will be working on independent projects most of the week.

The teacher will meet with the students twice a week to instruct, assign, and collect assignments that the students have completed on their own. This approach ensures accelerated progress, development of critical thinking abilities, student accountability for developing skills, and provides an enriched Whole Language core program, all within the regular classroom setting. This ought to be a comfortable, workable process for both the student and the teacher.

The areas of Math, Science, and Social Studies were purposefully excluded from this book. It is assumed that if children are gifted in Math, a text a grade level or two above the regular class's text will be provided. This effectively meets their needs. As for Science and Social Studies—gifted children learn best from the regular classroom programs. The traditional concepts and activities taught in these areas are important for them to know, and are essential in their social development as well. Everyone benefits from this approach. It strengthens interpersonal skills and relationships and bonds the class into a cohesive whole.

In keeping with Renzulli's definition, the "Gifted/Talented Indicator" on the following page was devised. As the name suggests, it is an informal profile meant to help teachers identify students who would benefit from a differentiated independent study program. NOTE: Though twenty-three separate behaviors are listed, a student need only exhibit eight or more to qualify for a differentiated curriculum.

This indicator is not intended to replace established standardized tests. It was created as an informal identification tool to assist teachers who do not have immediate access to psychologists who do such assessments.

If a student reveals a gifted/talented profile on this instrument, the instructor should seek formal testing for the child. While a psychologist's analysis is pending, the student will receive the differentiated curriculum she desperately needs. Even if the child doesn't formally test as gifted, he may still benefit from the independent study program.

GIFTED/TALENTED INDICATOR

Student's Name: _____ Date: _____

Mark the behaviors that best describe the child.

____	1.	Is an avid reader.
____	2.	Is outstanding in science, math, or literature.
____	3.	Has a wide range of interests.
____	4.	Is anxious to try new things.
____	5.	Seems very alert and gives rapid answers.
____	6.	Is self-motivated, needs little outside control.
____	7.	Tends to dominate peers or situations.
____	8.	Has self-confidence.
____	9.	Is sensitive to situations or the feelings of others.
____	10.	Can solve problems ingeniously.
____	11.	Has creative thoughts, ideas, or innovations.
____	12.	Is anxious to complete tasks.
____	13.	Has a great desire to excel.
____	14.	Is very expressive verbally.
____	15.	Tells imaginative stories.
____	16.	Has a mature sense of humor.
____	17.	Is inquisitive, takes a close look at things.
____	18.	Can show relationships between apparently unrelated things or ideas.
____	19.	Shows excitement about discoveries and is eager to share them.
____	20.	Tends to lose awareness of time.
____	21.	Is adept with art of visual expression.
____	22.	Exhibits body/facial gestures that are very expressive.
____	23.	Likes to work alone.

TOTAL ____ (If eight or more, put student in the gifted group.)

10

CHAPTER 2

BLOOM'S TAXONOMY

Higher thinking levels need to be incorporated into the curriculum to meet the needs of the gifted and talented students so they can think about problems instead of parroting answers. Bloom's Taxonomy is chosen for its simplicity and adaptability to learning activities. It has also been widely used and accepted in gifted circles.

Benjamin Bloom and others formulated a hierarchy of cognitive skills ranging from most basic cognitive skills to most advanced. Bloom stated that the greatest importance of the taxonomy is in its application to the classroom, where a teacher could consider the categories when planning the curriculum or choosing specific learning activities.

The categories are listed below as Bloom defined them:

1 KNOWLEDGE

The remembering of previously learned material. This may involve recall of a wide range of material, but all that is required is bringing to mind the appropriate information. Knowledge represents the lowest level of learning in the cognitive domain.

2 COMPREHENSION

The ability to understand the meaning of material. Interpreting material by explaining or summarizing it is an example of comprehension, which is the lowest level of understanding.

3 APPLICATION

The ability to use learned material in new, concrete situations. This may include the application of such things as rules, methods, concepts, principles, laws, and theories. Learning in this area requires a higher level of understanding than does comprehension.

4 ANALYSIS

The ability to break down material into its parts so that its structure may be understood. This may include the identification of the parts, analysis of the relationships between parts, or recognition of the organization involved. Learning, here, represents a higher intellectual level than do comprehension and application because it requires an understanding of both the content and the structural form of the material.

5 SYNTHESIS

The ability to put parts together to form a new whole. This may involve the production of a unique communication (theme or speech), a plan of operations (research proposal), or a set of abstract relations (scheme for classifying information). Learning in this area stresses creative behavior with major emphasis on forming new patterns.

6 EVALUATION

The ability to judge the value of material for a given purpose. The judgments are to be based on definite criteria. These criteria may be internal (organization of material) or external (material's relevance to a purpose), and the student may determine the criteria or be given the criteria. This level of thinking contains elements of all the other categories.

Though this model was not designed specifically for use with gifted children, the fact remains that these children often begin school with the ability to function at higher thinking levels. To preserve these abilities, the curriculum should contain activities that revolve around the upper levels of the taxonomy—Analysis, Synthesis, and Evaluation.

It has been suggested that students learn Bloom's Taxonomy in the classroom because it will make them aware of the higher thinking processes and they will consequently use them more often.

KNOWLEDGE	Remembering information.
COMPREHENSION	Understanding information.
APPLICATION	Using what is already learned in new situations.
ANALYSIS	Understanding all the parts.
SYNTHESIS	Putting the parts together into something new.
EVALUATION	Judging the value.

The chart above can be referred to by the teacher who wants to know which level is being exercised in a particular activity. Such a chart will also help a gifted child who is working on an independent project for which the teacher has required that only the upper three levels of the taxonomy be used (i.e., Analysis, Synthesis, and Evaluation).

To help teachers gear learning activities to thinking levels, a list of the verbs related to each level is provided on page 15. If a given learning activity is prefaced with one of these verbs, the corresponding level of Bloom's Taxonomy will be utilized.

KNOWLEDGE

Name	Outline	List
Describe	Select	Label
Define	Match	State

COMPREHENSION

Match	Extend	Locate
Generalize	Identify	Write
Give examples	Research	Explain

APPLICATION

Sketch	Change	Draw
Compute	Record	Operate
Solve	Apply	Use

ANALYSIS

Compare	Classify	Dissect
Survey	Advertise	Categorize
Separate	Analyze	Diagram
Select	Divide	Describe

SYNTHESIS

Create	Invent	Produce
Hypothesize	Design	Compose
Construct	Develop	Modify
Plan	Revise	Translate

EVALUATION

Defend	Decide	Predict
Debate	Determine	Suppose
Judge	Criticize	Summarize
Justify	Recommend	Support

EXAMPLES

KNOWLEDGE

"<u>Name</u> the states in New England."

COMPREHENSION

"<u>Match</u> the word with its definition."

APPLICATION

"<u>Sketch</u> the house as it is described in the story."

ANALYSIS

"<u>Compare</u> the two items; how are they similar and different?"

SYNTHESIS

"<u>Create</u> your own ending to the story."

EVALUATION

"<u>Defend</u> the character's point of view."

Teachers with gifted children in their classrooms need to pay particular attention to developing the upper three levels of Bloom's Taxonomy. By referring to these verbs, instructors can provide activities at the appropriate levels more easily. If the students also know them, they can suggest activities of their own.

WEEKLY SCHEDULE

This weekly schedule is designed to be easily integrated into any regular classroom program. The basic assumptions underlying this lesson plan are the following:

1. Four reading groups will exist — three regular groups (low, medium, high) and one gifted group.

2. Literature and writing will be integral parts of the gifted curriculum and regular curriculum.

3. The independent group will be working on independent assignments during the week.

The gifted reading group can consist of a group of students or a single child. The group meets twice a week — once on Monday to learn the assignments and review the material to be covered during the week, and again on Friday to turn in work, review it, and discuss any problems.

It is the instructor's job to make sure that the majority of the gifted group's work involves the upper levels of Bloom's Taxonomy, i.e., Analysis, Synthesis, and Evaluation. After the initial group meeting on Monday, reading, workbook, and spelling assignments are written on the board each day.

The remaining three reading groups and other subject areas covered by the other students continue unchanged. Altogether, the gifted group requires little more than an hour's worth of class time during an entire week, a small price to pay for a program that will infinitely enhance the abilities of the students and effect a positive atmosphere in the entire classroom.

All of the students in the gifted group will read works of literature for their reading instruction. One of the many positive side effects of this will be that many regular students will begin to check out the same books from the library and read them during silent reading time.

As interest in literature increases among the regular members of the class, the teacher can introduce excerpts from literature books into the regular reading groups, too. The instructor may even alternate between basal and literature books as a matter of course in the other reading groups. A general interest in literature will be one of the benefits of accommodating a gifted group in the regular classroom.

Caution should be exercised not to call undue attention to the abilities of the students in the gifted group. Avoid such practices as naming the group "Gifted" or any other word that would indicate its acceleration. The group should be given a name similar to the other group names.

On the following page is a suggested week's schedule for reading/ language arts.

WEEKLY SCHEDULE

Based on minimum of 1½ hours of Reading/Language Arts instruction daily.
Time allotments are approximates.

	MONDAY	TUESDAY	WEDNESDAY	THURSDAY	FRIDAY
	10-15 min. Opening: Roll, Lunch Count, etc.	Opening	Opening	Opening	Opening
	READING/ LANGUAGE ARTS 15 min - Read Aloud/ Instruction 45 min. - Writing Assignment (low rdg. if necessary) 30 min. - Gifted Group	READING/ LANGUAGE ARTS Read Aloud/Discuss 15 min. - Journal 20 min. Low Reading 20 min. Middle Reading 20 min. High Reading	READING/ LANGUAGE ARTS Read Aloud/Discuss Journal 20 min. Low Reading 20 min. Middle Reading 20 min. High Reading	READING/ LANGUAGE ARTS Read Aloud/Discuss Journal 20 min. Low Reading 20 min. Middle Reading 20 min. High Reading	READING/ LANGUAGE ARTS Read Aloud/Discuss Journal 20 min. Spelling 40 min. Literature Activities 20 min. Gifted Group
	MATHEMATICS 20 min. Read aloud	MATHEMATICS Read aloud	MATHEMATICS Read aloud	MATHEMATICS Read aloud	MATHEMATICS Read aloud
	SCIENCE / SOCIAL STUDIES / ART / MUSIC / P.E. / ETC.				
	10-30 min. Silent Reading	Silent Reading	Silent Reading	Silent Reading	Silent Reading
	Culminating Activities	Culminating Activities	Culminating Activities	Culminating Activities	Culminating Activities
	Dismissal	Dismissal	Dismissal	Dismissal	Dismissal

This week's schedule is based on a minimum of 1½ hours of reading/language arts instruction daily. It includes two opportunities to read aloud to students each day, journal writing, and silent reading. These activities are extremely important in developing reading and writing skills in all students.

Except for the gifted group meetings on Monday and Friday and the morning read-aloud time, this schedule resembles most regular classroom schedules.

Certain practices are scheduled daily or almost daily throughout the week.

Opening (10–15 minutes)

This includes taking roll, lunch counts, and other routine tasks the school requires.

Read Aloud/Discussion (15 minutes)

During this time, the teacher reads aloud from literature books, books of poetry, newspaper/magazine clippings, or even student stories. This is an informal time to discuss such topics such as author's purposes, mood/tone of the story, and students' reactions. Current events or even classroom projects can be discussed as they relate to the reading. Whatever topic is discussed will be applied to the writing assignment or journal writing that follows.

The only exception to this occurs on Monday when the reading will illustrate directly an important principle of writing (i.e., sentence/paragraph development, grammar, punctuation, etc.). After the reading, the teacher will give instruction on the writing principle for that day.

Journal Writing (15 minutes Tuesday–Friday)

This whole group assignment should be a natural outgrowth of the read aloud/discussion time. Students should be asked to do such things as:
- agree/disagree with author's point of view
- sequence the events of the story or project
- write their own original passages or poems which will invoke a mood/tone/dilemma, etc., similar to the author's
- compare/contrast characters to self or to another character students are familiar with

20

- give reactions to the topic
- list interview questions they would like to ask the author/character/person in the article
- write letters to the author/character/person in article
- forecast what might happen later in the story/article as a result of the action taken
- write sequels to the story
- write sentences or paragraphs about what was learned

These activities all stress the upper levels of Bloom's Taxonomy, but everyone in the class will benefit from employing them, not only the gifted students. All children need opportunities like these to express their ideas without worrying about right or wrong answers.

When reviewing the journal writing at the end of the week, spelling and punctuation should not be stressed. The ideas expressed are the only items of importance. Monday's writing lesson is the time when capitalization and punctuation and spelling should be stressed.

There will be more on this topic in the next chapter, "Writing and Journal Assignments."

Low/Medium/High Reading Groups

Continue providing regular instruction to the three traditional reading groups. Note that the low group meets up to four times a week, the middle and high groups meet three times a week, and the gifted group twice.

Mathematics

Continue math instruction as usual.

Lunch

Read Aloud

During this time the teacher reads exclusively out of literature books. Titles from the list in the Literature chapter (page 63) may be used.

Science/Social Studies/Art/Music/P.E., etc.

Continue instruction as usual.

Silent Reading

Silent reading is best when scheduled directly before or after a recess or P.E. Once the students become accustomed to the activity they will go into the classroom, get their respective books, and settle down comfortably to read. The teacher must settle back to read his or her own book, too. This way the students will see a good model.

The material the students will read depends entirely on what is established by the teacher. In most cases, material is limited to the students' library books, other books available in the classroom, or those brought from home. Friday can be a special silent reading day when class members are permitted to bring favorite comic or cartoon books and to share them quietly with a partner or two.

Culminating Activities

Those are the activities routinely done to conclude the day such as passing out papers, discussing homework assignments, and other class activities.

As the schedule shows, Monday and Friday are the two days that differ from the rest of the week; they are the days for meeting with the gifted students.

MONDAY

Opening

Read Aloud/Instruction (15 minutes)

This time should be spent reading excerpts from books, newspapers, and other sources that illustrate the concept around which the writing lesson will be structured. Have students give personal accounts related to the topic or at least generate some of their own ideas as a whole group or in small groups. The ideas created in this session will result in writing that is structured and much better organized than if the topic is given cold, without discussion.

Writing Assignment (45 minutes)

This assignment applies the language principles taught during the read aloud/instruction time preceding it. Ideas should be generated in the instruction period and many examples given so that students will understand the assignment, organize their thoughts, and be able to fully express themselves. The generous amount of time allows students to fully develop their ideas and to include detail in their writing.

The low reading group can be taken aside during the writing assignments so the teacher can help them formulate their ideas and put them on paper. Otherwise this group should be seen after the assignment is complete.

Gifted Group (30 minutes)

This is the first of two meetings with the gifted group during the week. Use this time to quickly review the day's assignments (these assignments should also be listed on the board daily). Have students skim the assigned chapter in their literature book or read specific paragraphs for a designated purpose which is listed on the board. Give instructions as needed.

The assignments given throughout the week are due on Friday. The remainder of the week the students will work independently or in small groups, completing the daily assignments.

FRIDAY

Read Aloud/Discussion

Read-aloud time can last longer than usual so that the book or story will come to a logical conclusion. The literature activities should be open-ended enough to revolve around the book or books the gifted students have been reading during the week.

Journal Writing

Continue Journal writing as usual.

Spelling (20 minutes)

Give the spelling test to the whole group, giving all the words in the standard spelling program. Gifted students should take these words, too. Then give the words on the gifted list. Those students who aren't in the gifted group can take the gifted words for extra credit if they wish. Otherwise, they can sit quietly and review their own words until the test is over. More detail is given about the spelling program in the chapter on Spelling (page 71).

Learning Activities

The remainder of Friday morning should include literature activities. This time is valuable because it integrates basic and critical thinking skills with literature and writing in an enjoyable way. To organize properly, the students have a few choices. For example, on a given Friday small groups can choose from three activities such as these:

1. PUPPETS — Make puppets, write a dialogue or story line, and practice and perform a puppet show, re-creating the book or story.
2. COOKING— Create a recipe that applies to the reading.
3. PREDICTING OUTCOMES — Write and illustrate a prediction of what will happen next in the story.

More activities are discussed in the chapter "Literature Activities and Recommended Books" (page 63).

Gifted Group (30 minutes)

As the rest of the class settles into their Friday activities the teacher will call up the gifted group and collect the week's work. Use this time to discuss the chapters that have been read and any concerns the students may have. Then suggest some enjoyable literature activities for each person in the group to do for the remainder of the morning. Allow them to choose different activities from those listed if they wish.

WRITING & JOURNAL ASSIGNMENTS

W riting is an activity engaged in every day. On Mondays it revolves around a single concept in the formal writing assignment. During the rest of the week the writing activity is an informal journal assignment for which the students will generate their own ideas. The gifted students will do the journal writing assigned to the entire class, then they will do another writing assignment linked to their daily independent reading.

MONDAY WRITING ASSIGNMENTS

This formalized writing assignment is preceded by a read-aloud or instruction time where passages clearly illustrating the principle to be taught are read. During the instruction time, the teacher should give numerous examples of the skill to make sure the students understand it before they begin.

Monday's writing assignment should include:

- Basic skills
- Summarizing
- Poetry
- Paragraph development
- Creative writing

All of these concepts are best learned when they can be used and applied in the context of full sentences or paragraphs. Traditional worksheets dealing with isolated concepts of grammar rules or punctuation rarely carry over into the students' writing. By teaching these concepts and having the class use them immediately in their writing, they are automatically learned and applied to other writing, too.

BASIC SKILLS

Basic writing skills are important for all students to learn and use. Though gifted students usually learn them in less time than regular students do, they can still profit from the experience. The important skills to know are:

- Punctuation
- Grammar
- Nouns, verbs, adjectives, adverbs
- Subject/predicate
- Capitalization
- Letter form—personal and business

A lesson on the use of adjectives might proceed as follows:
Read-Aloud: Chapters 11 and 12 of *Charlotte's Web*. Ask students to listen for descriptive words—adjectives.

Instruction: Give many examples of adjectives. Have the students give examples of sentences with adjectives and write them on the board.
EXAMPLES:
The large, round cat is lying on the blue rug.
Every green car goes down the bumpy, winding road.

Assignment: Write six sentences using as many adjectives as you can to describe characters in *Charlotte's Web*.

When correcting the writing assignment, it is best to correct only for the skill taught. If the assignment involves adjectives, correct only for adjectives; do not mark for spelling, punctuation, or anything else. Because writing is such a personal expression, the more specifically the skill is taught and corrected, the more comfortable students become in utilizing that skill.

It is important to remember that these skills provide a means to an end, they are not ends in themselves. The reason they are taught is so they can be applied to the student's general writing. Once they are learned, attention should be directed to the higher-level concepts of paragraph development: summarizing, creative writing, and poetry.

PARAGRAPH DEVELOPMENT

Semantic mapping is a good way to introduce basic paragraph organization. The map lends itself best to factual stories—it allows students to see a visual pattern of the information in the story. This allows them to see clusters of thoughts that can be combined into sentences and paragraphs. It is best to begin mapping as an activity involving the entire group. To start, simply choose a topic, read a selection on it, and write down the features that you wish to cover.

Activity: Semantic Mapping

Read-Aloud: Chapters 13–14 of *Island of the Blue Dolphins*.

Instruction: Before reading, have major headings listed on board. (*Cows — Looks, Behavior; Bulls — Looks, Behavior*). Tell students to listen to what cow and bull seal elephants look like and how they behave. After reading the chapters, students will give responses, which will be listed on the board. The semantic map may look like this:

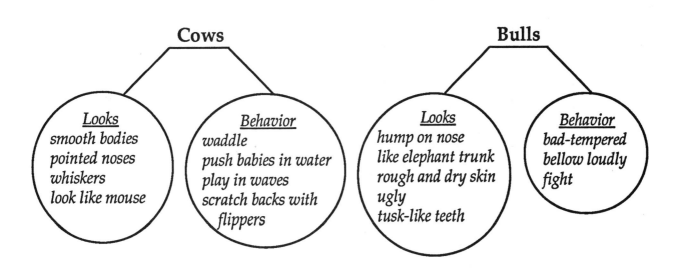

SEA ELEPHANTS

Cows

Bulls

Looks
smooth bodies
pointed noses
whiskers
look like mouse

Behavior
waddle
push babies in water
play in waves
scratch backs with
    flippers

Looks
hump on nose
like elephant trunk
rough and dry skin
ugly
tusk-like teeth

Behavior
bad-tempered
bellow loudly
fight

Have students dictate a paragraph about the cows and write it on the board.

EXAMPLE:

Sea Elephant Cows

The skin of a cow is smooth and her nose is pointed with whiskers. In many ways she looks like a mouse. She spends her days waddling along the shore and playing in the waves. When she has a baby, she teaches it to swim by pushing it into the water.

Assignment: Write a paragraph about bull sea elephants. Illustrate your paragraph when you are done.

(NOTE: Illustrating the paragraph helps the students visualize the information they've written down. We take illustration activities out of the curriculum too early—they can be used so constructively.)

Over time, this concept can be expanded to include report organization. In formulating a report on a subject like sea elephants, the students would do a semantic map of four or five aspects of the animal (habitat, food, looks, behavior), then string together paragraphs about each of those aspects. This approach encourages true reading comprehension and original writing instead of the plagiarizing from reference books that is so common.

SUMMARIZING

A story frame is a great way to teach summarizing in digestible doses. It divides a story into sections, making it easier to understand. A simple story frame divides the story into the beginning, middle, and end, and deals with the characters, setting, and plot of the story.

Activity: Summarizing with a Story Frame.

Read-Aloud: *The Giving Tree* by Shel Silverstein, or a newspaper/ magazine article (something that can be read in a single sitting).

Instruction: Who were the characters? What was the setting of the story? The plot? Ask students to capsulate these three most important concepts (characters, setting, and plot) for the beginning, middle, and the end of the story. (This is a difficult step for many and may take some time at first, but they soon will catch on.)

	CHARACTER	SETTING	PLOT
BEGINNING	Tree Boy (young)	Under tree	1. Boy and tree are friends. 2. Boy plays with tree and eats fruit. 3. Boy and tree are happy.
MIDDLE	Tree Boy (man)	With tree	1. Years go by and boy grows. 2. Boy wants money, house, and a boat. 3. Tree gives apples, branches, and trunk to the boy.
END	Tree Boy (old man)	On stump	1. Boy comes as old, old man to tree stump. 2. Tree sad it has nothing more to give. 3. Boy sits on stump. Tree is happy.

Assignment: Write a paragraph summary of *The Giving Tree* from the story frame.

Chaining is another way to teach summarizing. Students dictate the chain of events in the story.

Activity: Summarizing with chaining.

Read-Aloud: *The Giving Tree* or newspaper/magazine article or other short passage.

Instruction: What happened in the story/passage? Students dictate capsulated events of the story and teacher chains them on the board:

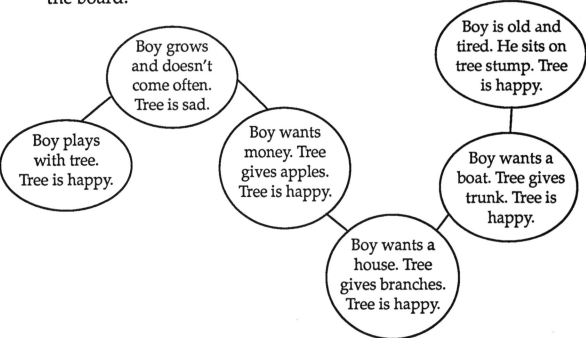

Assignment: Students write summary from chain of events.

CREATIVE WRITING

Once students are accustomed to using semantic maps, story frames, and chaining, they can use them to plot their own original stories. A stimulating way to begin creative writing is to depart from familiar stories by changing or omitting characters, changing the setting, or reorganizing the order of events.

Activity: Creative Writing

Read-Aloud (or retell): "Little Red Riding Hood."

Instruction: What might happen if Little Red Riding Hood were a grandmother going to visit her granddaughter? Teacher chains original student ideas on the board.

Assignment: Students choose one section of the chain and write a story about it or they can make up their own chain.

There are other variations on this idea.

1. Omit or add characters:
   - What if the wolf weren't in the story?
   - What if there were two rival wolves?

2. Rearrange the order of events:
   - What if Little Red Riding Hood were already at Grandma's?

3. Change the setting:
   - How would the story be different if it were on a beach?
   - Teacher reads a descriptive paragraph about a stormy night. Students write story using new setting.

4. Retell story from another character's point of view:
   - Tell "Little Red Riding Hood" from the wolf's point of view.

5. Tell what happened *before* the story started or *after* it ended.

Other creative writing activities may not depend on reading a story or passage. If that's the case, a great deal of discussion should take place. Listed are some enjoyable creative writing activities.

- Tell how to make a paper airplane (or any thing else that is relatively simple to do).
- Describe an object without naming it.
- Write down all the actions of someone or something in the room.
- Pretend you are a tetherball (or anything else). Describe your feelings during the day.
- Describe a day in the life of a pencil (other nouns can be used).
- Write a fairy tale in modern or futuristic terms.
- Invent a new machine; describe it.
- What would you put in a time capsule and why?
- Invent a new holiday and tell how it came to be and how it will be celebrated.
- Write an advertisement for a make-believe product.
- Imagine the history of a discarded item in the junk pile.
- Invent a new vitamin.
- Redesign a piece of clothing you're wearing and describe it.
- Rewrite your favorite nursery rhyme and substitute slang words.
- Analyze the qualities of a superhero.
- Classify yourself as a car (or any object) and describe your parts accordingly.

- Analyze what you would do if you were lost in the woods with nothing but the clothes you're wearing, a pocket knife, and a match.
- Write down a conversation between a cat and a dog (or any two people or animals).
- How are your parents the same as and different from you?
- Discuss the differences between cars and oranges (any two items can be substituted).
- Analyze the construction of a chair.
- Describe the special abilities that a ballet dancer needs (other nouns can be substituted).
- Describe the actions of an ant you are observing (other animals can be substituted).
- How does it feel to look down from a high place? Or from any precarious position?
- Describe a meeting between your teacher and Superman (or use any unlikely combination of two people).
- Criticize your favorite TV show.
- Recommend three things that will be essential for those living 25 years from now.
- Debate an issue by writing the pros and cons (handguns, smoking in public places, etc.).
- Write a note to put in a satellite to tell how good or bad Earth is.
- Is it a good idea to tell a secret? Why or why not?
- What is the most perfect place to be?
- What is the "good life"?
- What does generosity mean?
- Defend the idea that the earth is round.
- Describe your house from a visitor's point of view.

All these creative writing topics emphasize the use of the upper levels of Bloom's Taxonomy. Again, it is not only gifted students who will benefit from activities like these. They are enjoyable activities for everyone, and they stimulate the higher-order thinking skills in everyone.

Poetry

Assigning poetry-writing is an excellent way to challenge students creatively. Some of the many forms poetry can take are Haiku, Cinquain, and "Picture Poetry," which is a collection of letters, words, or phrases fashioned into the shape of an object.

Haiku

Haiku poetry consists of three lines. The first line contains five syllables, the second contains seven syllables, and the third line contains another five syllables.

Example:

From black ink escapes	(5 syllables)
the octopus, gig'ling	(7 syllables)
behind her surprise	(5 syllables)

Writing Haiku is an excellent way to reinforce the skill of syllabification in a creative and enjoyable manner.

Cinquain

Writing cinquain poetry is an excellent way to reinforce the concepts of nouns, adjectives, verbs, and synonyms. Though there are many variations of the structure of a cinquain poem, this version has four lines. The first line contains one word, a noun, and the second has two adjectives describing the noun. The third line contains three "-ing" verbs describing the actions of the noun, and the forth is a synonym for the initial noun.

Example:

Sunshine	(one noun)
Bright, yellow	(two adjectives)
Gleaming, glistening, blazing	(three verbs)
Daylight	(one synonym)

Picture Poetry

Fashioning free-form words or phrases into the shape of an object is an activity that uses the upper levels of Bloom's Taxonomy while reinforcing basic skills. One form of picture poetry is created by drawing an object lightly with pencil and writing phrases describing the object around the drawing. The pencil lines can be erased and the words will delineate the object.

Another variation of picture poetry is to make a picture out of a word.

Writing skills can be presented in a manner that is not tedious for either the teacher or the student. When writing becomes an integral part of the curriculum and is viewed as an enjoyable means of communication, students will continue to exercise it as a life skill.

DAILY JOURNAL WRITING

A journal is a place to record thoughts, similarities and differences, ascertain author's purpose, detect mood, and explore the inner workings of the book. It is a place to write freely without fear of correction. This form of expression is extremely important because there is a direct correlation between the amount of literature to which students are exposed and their writing abilities.

Monday is the day when the formalized mechanics of writing are taught and practiced; journal writing during the remainder of the week is intended solely for student expression. When expressing ideas, students should not worry too much about spelling, punctuation, etc.; if they do, the mechanics of writing will interfere with personal expression.

Any composition book or collection of bound writing paper can serve as a journal. Students should keep their journals handy so they can be easily retrieved for daily use. Unlike workbooks with pages of right and wrong answers, journals have no right/wrong answers. They are safe places to record ideas. Once students become accustomed to journal writing, they look forward to it every day.

Remember, all students will have a journal assignment after the read-aloud session in the morning. On top of that, the gifted group will have another journal assignment to complete each day as part of their independent reading.

It is best for the gifted group to have two separate journals—one for the whole class activities, one for their independent assignments. The same types of journal activities should be used with both assignments—the only difference will be the book that is being read.

Listed below and on the next page are journal activities that emphasize the upper levels of Bloom's Taxonomy.

DAILY JOURNAL ASSIGNMENTS

- List similarities and differences between yourself and (character).
- How are (character) and (character) the same? Different? Are they happy? Sad? Nervous? Calm? (Use any one of these categories or any others.)
- List the words the author uses to describe setting, mood, character, etc., then write your own description using similar words.
- What do you want to say to (character) to help him/her with this situation?
- Do you agree or disagree with (character's) decision? Explain.
- Draw a gift you would give to (character) and explain why you would give it to him or her.
- If you were in the character's situation, how would you feel? Why?
- Make up a new title for the chapter. Explain why you chose it.
- Compose a letter to (character) from (character's) point of view explaining his or her feelings about the situation.
- Rewrite the end of the chapter.

- Write a diary for (character) explaining the events in this chapter and his or her reactions to them.
- List interview questions you would want to ask (character).
- Make up dialogue between (character) and (character).
- List examples of similes and metaphors the author uses in this chapter. Make up some samples of each on your own.
- Draw how you think (character's) room would appear. Describe it.
- Add a new character to this chapter. Explain what would have happened if he or she were in the story.
- Create (character's) background—tell about events that may have happened before the story takes place that would explain his or her behavior.

Student journals should be collected regularly and read by the teacher. Of course the gifted group's journals will be collected on Friday. The journals of the rest of the class can be collected during their reading group, or also on Friday while the literature activities are going. Another technique is to collect half the class's journals one week and the other half the next week. Again, the only exception will be the gifted group, whose journals will be read weekly.

A journal should be filled with lists, letters, multiple endings, sketches with descriptions, poems, and original passages. In short, it should reflect an in-depth exploration of all aspects of the literature read.

Teacher comments should be confined to the content of the writing, nothing more. React to ideas, praise original thoughts, and suggest other reading material if appropriate.

Listed below is a week's worth of sample journal assignments for the gifted independent assignments. Though Monday's writing time is spent on formal writing assignments, the gifted group will still have a reading journal assignment that day. It will be discussed in reading group.

These assignments use the good lesson design of "before, during, and after" reading activities. It is assumed the teacher uses good lesson design with all reading, writing, and journal assignments.

SAMPLE JOURNAL ASSIGNMENTS FOR INDEPENDENT GIFTED GROUP

MONDAY

Before Reading: A gloomy beginning paragraph starts this book. List descriptive words you might use to describe something stormy and gloomy.

Read: Chapter 1, *A Wrinkle in Time* by Madeline L'Engle

Journal: Write your own paragraph describing a gloomy night.

Before Reading	Journal
dark petrified shocks of thunder bursts of lightening eerie cold	*It was a dark and stormy night. An eerie moon peeked through the black clouds as they billowed dark and cold around it. Soon the clouds clustered together, cloaking the night sky, and bursts of lightning flashed in crooked fingers piercing the night. Shocks of thunder rolled through the countryside. I was petrified.*

TUESDAY

Before Reading: Have you ever had feelings you couldn't understand? In this chapter, Meg talks about her feelings about her father.

Read: Chapter 2, *A Wrinkle in Time*

Journal: Pretend you are Meg. Write a letter to your father and try to explain your feelings about everything that's happening.

Dear Dad,

So much has been happening, I don't know where to begin. I worry about you and it makes me weird at school. That dumb old principal thinks you're not coming home, but I know you are. I know it!

These strange old ladies moved into the haunted house. Charles Wallace thinks they are part of some plan. I don't know what to think. It's all too confusing.

I'll be happy when you're home.

Love,

Meg

WEDNESDAY

Before Reading: List what you think are some important reasons to like someone and some unimportant reasons. In this chapter, Calvin talks of the reasons people like him.

Read: Chapter 3, *A Wrinkle in Time*

Journal: Write the important and unimportant reasons people like you.

Before Reading	Journal
Important Reasons	*Important Reasons*
Personality *Similar likes/dislikes*	*The important reasons people like me are these: my good sense of humor and my liking to talk to them. I also help people whenever I can.*
Unimportant Reasons	*Unimportant Reasons*
Looks *Popularity* *Good Athlete*	*The unimportant reasons people like me are these: I'm good in school and sometimes I help them with their homework. When they like me for these things, they like what I do, not who I am.*

THURSDAY

Before Reading: Draw what you think evil looks like. Write down what forms it might take. You encounter something evil in this chapter. Read about the form it takes.

Read: Chapter 4, *A Wrinkle in Time*

Journal: Draw the Black Thing. Why are your feelings about the Black Thing different from your feelings about Mrs. Which even though she wears black, too?

Before Reading:

Journal:

Mrs. Which is kind-hearted and trying to help. The Black Thing is a void that swallows everything in its path. It's like a bottomless pit that never fills up. It's not mean — it's just nothingness.

FRIDAY

Before Reading: Think about all of the feelings Meg had in chapters 1–4 of *A Wrinkle in Time*. Compare feelings you've had that are similar. Be prepared to discuss them.

LITERATURE ACTIVITIES:

1. **ACT IT OUT** — Dress up like one of the characters, then write and act out the role, telling who you are and what's happened to you.

2. **DIARY** — Write a diary of one of the characters up to this point in the story.

3. **MAP** — Draw a map of Meg's house and surrounding area. Label the haunted house and school and other things mentioned in the book.

GIFTED READING GROUP

The gifted reading group will meet twice a week, once on Monday and again on Friday. On Monday the spelling words and week's work are discussed and Monday's reading/journal assignment is given. On Friday all the week's assignments are collected.

Students in the gifted reading group should be given a minimum assignment of one chapter a day to read in their literature books. This can be adjusted if the chapters are unusually long and difficult or short. (Specific books and culminating assignments are discussed in the Literature Chapter, which begins on page 63.)

Make sure to use good reading-lesson design when assigning the gifted group's tasks. Every lesson should contain:

1. a **before-reading** activity to get the students personally involved in the story,
2. a **purpose-for-reading** activity supplying a specific point for which the students must read, and
3. an **after-reading** activity which involves writing in a journal.

These activities do not have to be elaborate or take up too much time, but they should be used for every reading assignment, whether in Monday's group meeting or for daily board assignments.

BEFORE-READING ACTIVITIES

Some excellent before-reading activities are:

- Discussion
- Drawing/writing own ideas
- Semantic mapping
- Predicting outcomes

The examples given below are before-reading activities that fall into the "purpose for reading" category.

DISCUSSION

Discussion can be done during group meetings on Mondays or in pairs or clusters as independent activity during the week.

Before Reading: In pairs or clusters discuss some ways you would solve Mrs. Frisby's problem. List them. Mrs. Frisby could:

- Go to the farmer and ask him not to plow. • Ask for help.
- Take a chance and move Timothy.   • Sabotage the tractor.

Read: Chapters 7 and 8 of *Mrs. Frisby and the Rats of NIMH*. Read what Mrs. Frisby does about her problem.

DRAWING/WRITING OWN IDEAS

This is the most prevalent before-reading activity during the week since the gifted students are working independently on their assignments.

Before Reading: If you were Mrs. Frisby, what are some questions you would ask of Mr. Ages? Write them down. Example:

1. *What can you do for me that I can't do for myself?*
2. *Why is my dead husband important?*
3. *Will Timothy survive the move?*

Read: Chapters 11 and 12 of *Mrs. Frisby and the Rats of NIMH*. See which of your questions are answered.

SEMANTIC MAPPING

This can be done individually or in pairs or clusters. Students enjoy this activity very much, but care should be taken not to use it more often than once a week so that the novelty won't wear off. Semantic mapping is best suited to factual information, but can be adapted to certain kinds of fiction.

Before Reading: Map what you would use for shelter and food if you went to live alone in the woods.

Shelter	Food
lean-to of branches	nuts
cave	berries
bushes	fish

Read: Chapters 1–4 of *My Side of the Mountain.* See what Sam does about shelter and food. Add and delete ideas from your map.

PREDICTING OUTCOMES

Predicting outcomes is an excellent way for students to apply their knowledge of character analysis and conflict resolution to a story. It is best used in key situations where the character is challenged somehow. Again, there are no right or wrong answers when predicting outcomes. As long as the students can justify their answers, any are acceptable.

Before Reading: What do you think Shirley would do if someone hurt her? Write down what you think she would do and why.
Example:
She'll tell her parents, who will talk to the teacher.

Read: "May-Two Black Eyes and Wispy Whiskers" from *In the Year of the Boar and Jackie Robinson.* See what Shirley does.

PURPOSE FOR READING

As illustrated above, the purpose for reading gives the students something specific to look for. This enhances comprehension and the quality of the journal-writing after-reading activity tremendously. Every student benefits from this lesson design, but gifted students are particularly stimulated by it. It challenges their analytical and critical thinking skills and prompts extremely original writing.

AFTER–READING ACTIVITIES

The after-reading activity should follow up the ideas generated in the before-reading activity. Some of the most effective strategies are:

- Discussion
- Drawing/writing own ideas
- Semantic mapping
- Chaining
- Story frame

Note that many of these activities were discussed in-depth in the "Writing and Journal Assignments" Chapter. They lend themselves well to many reading and writing activities.

DISCUSSION

The natural followup to listing ways Mrs. Frisby could solve her problem in *Mrs. Frisby and the Rats of NIMH* is for the students to compare their answers to what Mrs. Frisby actually did in the chapters. Even if their answers differ, they are acceptable (as long as they can defend them).

In their pairs or clusters they should discuss and defend their answers, and then record the results of the discussion in their journals.

Example:

Mrs. Frisby could:
- *Go to the farmer and ask him not to plow.*
  But the farmer wouldn't believe it if a mouse talked to him.

- *Sabotage the tractor.*
  But the farmer could quickly fix it.

- *Take a chance by moving Timothy.*
  But it will put Timothy's life in danger.

- *Ask for help.*
  The rats could help her.

DRAWING/WRITING IDEAS

Again, this will be the most common assignment for the independent gifted group.

The next step in the assignment is to ascertain which questions were answered and how they were answered.

Example:

1. *What can you do for me that I can't do for myself?*
   Answered: Rats have technology and other abilities.

2. *Why is my dead husband important?*
   Answered: Jonathan helped the rats a lot but was killed in the line of duty. They wish to pay him back by helping his wife and children.

3. *Will Timothy survive the move?*
   Answered: The rats can help with the move so it won't be hard on Timothy. Only time will tell whether or not he survives.

SEMANTIC MAPPING

After students have completed their before-reading semantic map, they go back to it, circle likely answers, and add more as the story suggests.

Example:

Shelter	**Food**		
hollowed-out tree	*nuts*	*turtle soup*	*arrow-leaf*
lean-to of branches	*berries*	*acorn pancakes*	*venison*
cave	*fish*	*mussels*	*small game*
bushes		*cattails*	

CHAINING

This is great fun and the students always enjoy it. After reading the assigned chapter, they are asked to alter one of the major events and brainstorm what might happen next.

Use some of the ideas the students came up with when predicting outcomes as a before-reading activity.

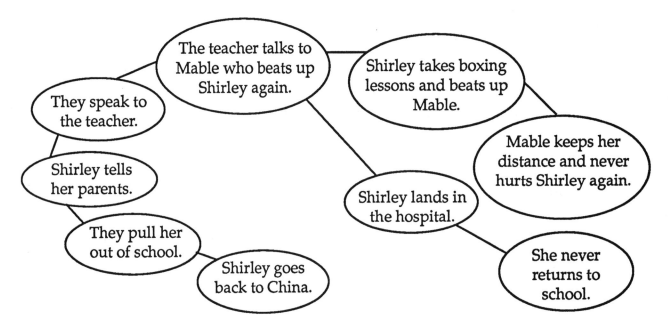

46

STORY FRAME

This is a good way to summarize the events of the chapter or of the entire book. Divide the chapter or book into three sections marked beginning, middle, and end. Then place characters, setting, and plot across the top of the chart and fill them in.

For a section of *Tuck Everlasting* by Natalie Babbit, the story frame would look like this.

	CHARACTER	SETTING	PLOT
BEGINNING	Jessie Tuck Miles Tuck Mae Tuck Winnie Foster	on the road	The Tucks explain about their drinking water from a special spring 187 years ago. It stopped their aging. They kidnapped Winnie because she saw where the spring was.
MIDDLE	Jessie Miles Mae Winnie Stranger	on the road	Unknown to everyone, a stranger overheard their amazing story and followed them home.
END	Miles Mae Angus Winnie	Tuck's house	Winnie and the Tucks arrive home at the Tucks' house, where the boys go swimming. Mrs. Tuck greets Winnie in a friendly way.

A good way to finish the study of a book is to use an interesting and enjoyable report form employing all the upper levels of Bloom's Taxonomy. The next few pages contain such a report form.

BOOK REPORT FORM

The levels of Bloom's Taxonomy reinforced by each activity on this form are indicated with these abbreviations:

K Knowledge   **An** Analysis

C Comprehension   **Syn** Synthesis

Ap Application   **Eval** Evaluation

Name _____

Book Title _____

Author _____

An : Why do you think the author gave the book this title?

_____

_____

_____

Syn : Think of another title for this book. Why did you choose it?

_____

_____

_____

Ap : Design a cover for this book.
Explain why you chose this design.

Syn : Think of a present you could give one of the characters.
Draw it on the page below, describe it, and tell why
you would give it.

_____

_____

_____

An : Which character is most like you? How?

_____

_____

An : Which character is least like you? How?

_____

_____

Eval : What happens in the story that you wish could happen to you? Why?

_____

_____

_____

An : What subject does this book make you want to learn more about? Why?

_____

_____

Ap : List some sources where you could research this topic.

_____

_____

Eval : Imagine you are a literary critic. Write your honest opinion of this book. Be concerned with not only the plot and characters but with the author's style and development of the story.

_____

_____

_____

_____

_____

_____

_____

_____

_____

_____

_____

Syn : Design an advertisement for this book on a separate sheet of paper to use in a magazine. Use black and three other colors. Make sure the layout is neat and easy to read.

SEATWORK/ DAILY ASSIGNMENTS

Too often gifted students are asked to do two to three times the number of workbook pages and duplicated worksheets that average students do. Not only is this a waste of time for the gifted students to complete and the teacher to correct, it leaves the student with the unpleasant idea that he or she is to work harder than everyone else on the same dull, repetitive material. This can quickly lead to burn-out, with the gifted child failing to apply him- or herself to any task for fear of being given an extra bulk of low thinking level work to do once the task is complete.

To avoid this it is important to use seatwork effectively in ways that will appropriately challenge gifted students without leaving the teacher exhausted from the strain of extra correcting or leaving the student overloaded with repetitive work. Depending on worksheets to deliver the bulk of the gifted curriculum demands a disproportionate amount of teacher time. Use seatwork effectively by choosing good, appropriate assignments, and adjust workbook assignments by applying the following concepts.

Adjusting Workbook Assignments

The teacher should choose workbook assignments carefully. This kind of seatwork can be a valuable learning tool when properly utilized, but too often it consists of useless worksheets that require filling in the blanks or giving a single correct answer. These kinds of activities require little higher-level thinking and serve no educational purpose for the gifted student.

Since the gifted group is primarily engaged in independent work, the work assigned should be of good quality. Worksheets stressing upper-level thinking skills are readily available in every basal program but it is up to the teacher to seek them out and use them.

It is wise to put gifted students into workbooks that are not tied to specific events in the stories of the basal reading series. The workbooks should be a grade level or two above the actual grade level of the students. Though gifted students can master basic skills in much less time than average students, it is still important to provide practice in these skills.

Worksheet Considerations

Consider these three things when giving a workbook assignment to gifted as well as regular students:

1. OMIT — activities in which the student is asked to circle or fill in the blanks without much thought.
2. EXTEND — activities in which the skill is important but the worksheet is simplistic, by assigning another activity that uses the basic concept of the page.
3. KEEP — any assignment that asks comprehension questions, calls for making inferences, drawing conclusions, predicting outcomes, or establishing cause/effect relationships.

On the following pages you will find sample activities and recommendations to OMIT, EXTEND, or KEEP.

EXAMPLE:

> ### Verbs - Action Words
>
> Verbs tell what is happening in the sentence.
>   Joseph **built** a large sandcastle.
>   It **washed** out to sea.
>
> Write the action word that tells what is happening in the sentence.
>
> 1. Wilbur and Orville Wright designed an early airplane.
>
> 2. It flew a short distance.
>
> 3. Today planes travel thousands of miles.

OMIT - Skill is too simplistic. Instead, have students write five sentences using action verbs and underline them.

EXAMPLE:

> Complete each sentence with a word from the box.
>
> | delicate | correction | exercise | rotate |
> |----------|------------|----------|--------|
> | exact | valid | estimate | triumphant |
>
> 1. Julie held up the thin fabric and exclaimed over its _____ pattern.
>
> 2. Because her library card was not _____, Connie could not check out any books.
>
> 3. Fresh air and _____ help people stay healthy.
>
> 4. The team cheered at their _____ victory.

OMIT - Low-level comprehension task using vocabulary. Instead, have students use words correctly in their own sentences **(application).**

EXAMPLE:

Circle the pieces of clothing.
Draw a line under the plants.
Put an "X" on the animals.

OMIT - Skill is good but exercised at a lower thinking level. Instead, have students make the categories and list things under each, thus converting it to an **analysis** activity.

EXAMPLE:

Read each statement. Choose the word that best describes the speaker's feelings. Write it under the sentence.

confident   confused   bored   irritated

1. "There are so many trails to hike; I cannot decide which one to take." _____

2. "Will you please wait your turn? I was here first." _____

3. "I know I will do well at the speech tournament."

_____

EXTEND - This is a good **comprehension** skill. Assign half the page, then have students write their own statements showing each emotion. This extends the activity so that it becomes an **application** activity.

EXAMPLE:

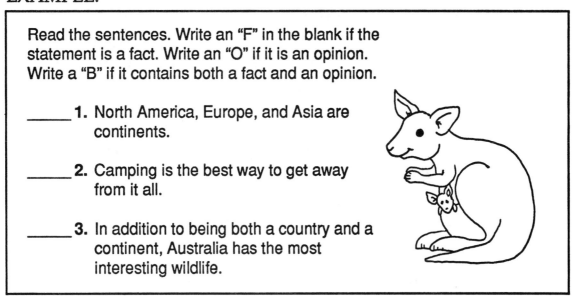

Read the sentences. Write an "F" in the blank if the statement is a fact. Write an "O" if it is an opinion. Write a "B" if it contains both a fact and an opinion.

_____ 1. North America, Europe, and Asia are continents.

_____ 2. Camping is the best way to get away from it all.

_____ 3. In addition to being both a country and a continent, Australia has the most interesting wildlife.

EXTEND - It is a good **comprehension** skill that can be extended to the **application** and **analysis** levels if students create their own fact and opinion statements.

EXAMPLE:

Read to decide if the bold word is used correctly in each sentence. Write "yes" if it is correct, "no" if it is not correct.

_____ 1. When people set a meeting time it is called a **routine**.

_____ 2. A **podiatrist** works on people's feet.

_____ 3. To **account** for your actions means no one cares what you do.

_____ 4. A **mercantile** is a general store.

EXTEND - This **knowledge/comprehension** skill should be assigned in part and extended to an **application** activity by students' using the words correctly in their own sentences.

EXAMPLE:

Propaganda is a powerful way of getting a point across. Read each passage and write the letter of the propaganda technique being used.

A. Bandwagon   C. Repetition
B. Testimonial   D. Emotional Words

_____ 1. Swimming champion Dave Larson says, "I used to be exhausted after practice until I started taking Vibrant Vitamins. If you take them, you will have the energy to make you a champion, too."

_____ 2. Are you tired at the end of the day because you have been slaving away? Vibrant Vitamins let you reawaken to the vitality of life and be a zombie no more. Take them at the start of your day, and put some zip into that zombie!

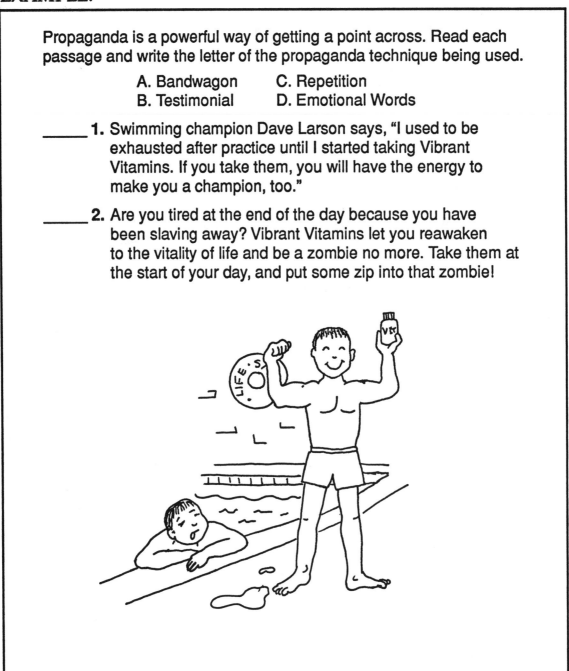

EXTEND - This **comprehension/analysis** skill is excellent and can be extended to the **application** level by having students write their own examples of each technique.

EXAMPLE:

Read the paragraph below and complete the chart. Put a check under the name of the person who fits the description.

Jenny and Jocko make kites. Jenny has been involved in designing and flying kites for over four years. Recently she got Jocko involved; now they spend weekends together testing their new designs. Jenny thinks of the shapes and colors the new kites will be. She draws them on paper, noting the size of each piece and the material of which it should be made. Jocko puts them together according to her specifications. Once the work is done, the fun begins. Together Jenny and Jocko fly their creations and watch them soar.

	Jenny	Jocko
love/loves kites		
has/have spent four years involved with kites		
put/puts kites together according to specifications		
fly/flies new kite creations		

KEEP - An excellent **analysis** activity - no extensions necessary unless students look for other similarities and differences not mentioned.

EXAMPLE:

After reading the passage, fill in the circle beside the best answer.

Carlos and Cathy were playing a quiet game when something happened that made Cathy smile. She nudged Carlos and showed him what happened. He smiled, too. As the game continued, funny things kept happening, and Carlos and Cathy put their hands over their mouths as their eyes danced with laughter.

Which sentence is probably true according to the facts in the story?

○ a. Carlos and Cathy do not like each other.

○ b. Carlos and Cathy were trying to keep from laughing out loud.

○ c. Carlos and Cathy do not play well together.

○ d. Carlos and Cathy were making too much noise.

KEEP - This calls for making inferences, which is a high **comprehension/ application** skill requiring some **evaluation** on the part of the student.

EXAMPLE:

Read the paragraph and write what you think will happen next and why.

Tomasita watched as the boat pulled away from the shore. Though she had known for some time her mother had to leave, it was very difficult now that it was actually happening. As she wiped the tears from her eyes and looked again toward her mother in the boat, something seemed odd. Instead of waving good-bye, Tomasita's mother waved with an urgency that had not been there a moment before.

_____

_____

_____

_____

KEEP - Any page asking students to predict outcomes asks them to function at a **synthesis** and **evaluation** level.

EXAMPLE:

Carefully read each paragraph below. List three things discussed in the article that were similar and different, then list their similarities and differences.

Eskimos in the frozen Arctic are known for a temporary structure they build from the ice and snow called an igloo. Fashioned into a circular shape, it serves as a comfortable shelter when away from the village on prolonged hunting expeditions. The ice serves as insulation and reflects heat created by the fire in the center of the structure. A hole in the top of the dome in the igloo allows smoke to escape but lets little of the cold from the outside in. As a result, the occupants stay very comfortable.

Pioneers who lived on the plains built a permanent shelter out of materials nature provided. It was made from squares of sod cut from the ground and stacked to form a square-shaped structure. Smoke from the central fire escaped from a hole in the roof while the sod acted as insulation keeping the inhabitants warm. Many a pioneer survived a harsh winter in the comfort provided by a simple sod house.

What things are compared and contrasted?	Similarities	Differences
1. _____	1. _____	1. _____
	_____	_____
	_____	_____
	_____	_____
2. _____	2. _____	2. _____
	_____	_____
	_____	_____
	_____	_____
3. _____	3. _____	3. _____
	_____	_____
	_____	_____
	_____	_____

KEEP - This is an excellent example of an **analysis** activity requiring a great deal of comprehension and critical thinking.

EXAMPLE:

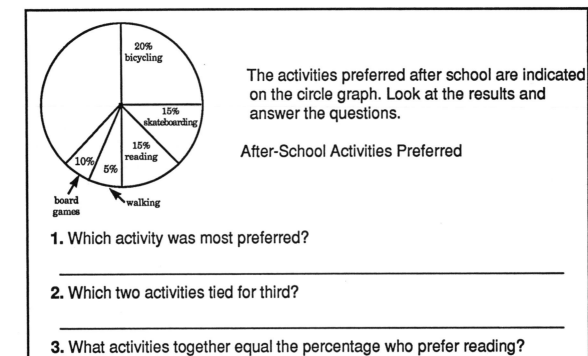

The activities preferred after school are indicated on the circle graph. Look at the results and answer the questions.

After-School Activities Preferred

1. Which activity was most preferred?

_____

2. Which two activities tied for third?

_____

3. What activities together equal the percentage who prefer reading?

_____

4. What percentage of activities can be done sitting down? What are they?

_____

5. What conclusions can you draw from the graph results?

_____

KEEP - Any graph or map interpretation activity requires **analytical** and **evaluative** thinking. This can be extended by students taking their own polls and making their own graphs which would call for **synthesis.**

Remember, the teacher should make the final decision on which worksheets to assign. Once the instructor has decided a worksheet is suitable, it can then be extended by applying the skill in another way.

By extending assignments the teacher not only reduces the amount of paperwork to correct but causes students to exercise their higher thinking abilities, the desired result of all instruction.

LITERATURE ACTIVITIES AND RECOMMENDED BOOKS

Friday is the day to culminate the reading done during the week. The entire class will be engaged in choosing from approximately three activities which might range from putting on puppet shows and constructing models to preparing food eaten by characters from the reading materials.

The gifted group should also engage in the activities that relate to what they have read throughout the week. But they should also have the option of creating their own projects. Some may choose to write a sequel or a prologue to the reading, or may choose some other ambitious activity which would better suit their interests and talents.

For example, students may choose from these literature activities:
- BOOK COVER—Create a book cover for the book/story.
- RADIO ADVERTISEMENT—Write and tape-record (or perform) a radio advertisement that will make people want to read the story.
- MAP—Make a map of the area where the story took place. Indicate where each event occurred, and be sure to include a key.

These activities involve all aspects of language arts: reading, writing, listening, and speaking. In many cases, students will return to the stories or books to get more information for their projects. Even if some of these projects seem minor, they all involve a great deal of thinking and employ the upper levels of Bloom's Taxonomy.

Listed below are a number of popular activities to use with the stories. On the surface they may appear to be fun and games — in actuality, they utilize upper level thinking skills.

- PLAY: Write and perform a play based on the story.
- READ/RECORD: Tape-record the story (or your favorite part of the book) in your best reading voice, adding sound effects.
- DIARY: Write a diary for one of the characters telling what happened to him or her.
- PANTOMIME: Pantomime the story (or your favorite part of the story).
- TIMELINE: Make a timeline of the events of the story. Explain it.
- TV COMMERCIAL: Write and perform a TV commercial to sell the book.
- DRESS-UP: Dress up like one of the characters and tell what happened to him or her.
- COMIC BOOK: Make a comic book based on the book.
- LISTENING POST: Listen to students reading favorite parts of the book.
- BOOK COVER: Create a book cover for the story. Explain it.
- DRAWINGS: Make a series of five drawings depicting the major points. Describe them.
- NEW CHARACTER: Create another character for the story. Tell how things would change with this character's presence.
- AUTHOR BIOGRAPHY: Research and prepare an oral report on the author's life.
- REWRITE STORY: Rewrite your favorite part of the book using yourself as a character and a favorite place as the setting.
- FILMSTRIP: Create a filmstrip of the story. Describe each frame as you show it.
- ROLL MOVIE: Draw a series of pictures depicting events in the books and an example of each on shelf paper. Make a "roll movie" of the story. Explain the story as you show it.

- BOOK DISPLAY: Put together a display of other books the author has written. Tell about them.

- RADIO ADVERTISEMENT: Write and tape-record a radio advertisement that will make people want to read the story.

- NEW ENDING: Create a new ending for the story. Explain why it is better than the original.

- QUILT: Make a friendship quilt of the story. Each student sews or draws a square depicting an incident from the book. As a class, sequence them together into a quilt.

- POSTER: Create a poster advertising the book. Explain it.

- TEN QUESTIONS: Play a game with others: Ask ten questions about a character in the book. By the end of the tenth question or before, they should guess the character.

- CROSSWORD PUZZLE: Construct a crossword puzzle of words and their definitions from the story.

- TO READ/NOT TO READ: Students give reasons to read and not to read the book.

- POEM: Write and illustrate a poem about the story.

- PUPPET SHOW: Perform a puppet show of the story.

- BUMPER STICKER: Make a bumper sticker advertising the story.

- NEWSPAPER: Design the front page of a newspaper with headlines and a story about what happened in the book.

- MOVIE POSTER: Draw a movie poster advertising the story, and cast a real actor in each character's role. Explain it.

- MOVIE CRITIC: Pretend you are a movie critic, and criticize the book as if it were a movie.

- MODEL: Construct a model of something used in the book. Describe it.

- INTERVIEW: Write and tape-record an interview with one of the characters in the story.

- DIORAMA: Make a diorama of your favorite part of the story; be prepared to tell about it.

- CHARACTER SKETCH: Sketch a portrait of a character and write (or tell) everything about him or her.

- MAP: Make a map of the area where the story took place. Indicate where each event occurred and be sure to include a key.

- DISPLAY: Make a display of items mentioned in the books. Explain their significance.

- WORD SEARCH: Design a word search puzzle using words from your story.

- DEMONSTRATION: Demonstrate how to make/do something learned from the story.

- SCRAPBOOK: Construct a scrapbook for your favorite character. Explain it.

- SINGING: Write out and sing songs mentioned in the book.

- GAME: Make up a gameboard (with written rules) based on your book.

- BULLETIN BOARD: Put together a bulletin board of the story. Label the parts.

- MURAL: Construct a mural about the book. Tell about it.

- PEEP BOX: Make a peep box scene from your book. Explain it.

- CLAY SCULPTURE: Create a clay sculpture of a scene or character from the book. Be prepared to explain it.

- CHILDREN'S BOOK: Write and illustrate a children's book summarizing the story for someone younger.

- CARVING: Do a soap or potato carving of something from the book.

- MOBILE: Construct a mobile of important things in the story with labels explaining each of them.

- COOKING: Prepare a recipe from something mentioned in the book.

- T-SHIRT DESIGN: Fashion a T-shirt advertising the book. Explain why you chose the design.

- COLLAGE: Put together a collage of the story from magazine pictures. Describe your collage.

- LIFE CYCLES: Study the life cycle of an animal mentioned in the story.

- LETTER FROM CHARACTER: Write a letter from a character to the reader explaining his or her actions in the book.

- LETTER TO CHARACTER: Write a letter to a character telling about your reaction to him or her in the book.

- PARODY: Write and perform a humorous parody of a scene in the story.

- MASK: Create a mask of one of the characters. Tell about it.

- COLLECTION: Make a collection of something mentioned in the book. Write about it.

- FLANNELBOARD STORY: Create and tell about a scene from the book.

- READ TO A FRIEND: Read your book (or a favorite part of the book) to a friend.

- PAINTING: Create and explain your painting of a scene from the story.

- BANNER: Using a length of shelf paper, design a banner advertising the book.

- GRAPH: Graph student reactions to critical decisions in the book.

- LETTER TO AUTHOR: Write a letter to the author giving your reactions to the book.

- FOLD BOOK: Make a fold book, writing and illustrating main events of the story. (To make a fold book, fold an 8½" x 11" sheet of paper in half, then in half again. Cut along the single folds, almost to the center, making a four–page book.)

- CHALK TALK: Give a brief account of the story, illustrating important points at the chalkboard.

- PUZZLE: Draw a scene from the story, cut the scene into puzzle pieces, and write a short summary.

- QUIZ: Make up a quiz of five to ten questions about the book. Have others who read the book take the quiz.

- RIDDLES: Make up riddles about specific characters. Write them down.

- RETELL STORY: Explain how story would have been different if some major event had happened differently.

- DECORATE DOOR: Decorate the classroom door like the cover of a book.

- CLASS NEWSPAPER: Compile and circulate a class newspaper.

Engaging in literature activities is an enjoyable way to integrate almost all aspects of reading.

A bibliography of quality books is listed below. These are all well-recognized books, and many have won awards or are considered classics in their fields. This list represents a good cross-section of subject matter, of cultural and human experiences.

Some of these books may also be used by the teacher during the daily read-aloud times.

BIBLIOGRAPHY

TITLES GRADES:	4	5	6	7	8
Adam of the Road, *Gray*		X	X	X	
Around the World in Eighty Days, *Verne*		X	X	X	X
Arthur, For the Very First Time, *MacLachlan*	X	X	X		
The Big Wave, *Buck*		X	X	X	X
Blue Willow, *Gates*	X	X			
Bridge to Terabithia, *Paterson*		X	X		
Call It Courage, *Sperry*	X	X	X		
The Cay, *Taylor*		X	X		
Charlotte's Web, *White*	X	X	X		
The Cricket in Times Square, *Selden*		X	X		
Dicey's Song, *Voight*				X	X
Dragonwings, *Yep*		X	X		
Freaky Friday, *Rodgers*		X	X	X	

TITLES GRADES:	4	5	6	7	8
From the Mixed-up Files of Mrs. Basil E. Frankweiler, *Konigsburg*		X	X		
The Great Brain, *Fitzgerald*		X	X		
The Hobbitt, *Tolkien*		X	X	X	X
I Heard the Owl Call My Name, *Craven*				X	X
The Incredible Journey, *Burnford*			X	X	X
The Indian in the Cupboard, *Banks*			X	X	X
Jacob Have I Loved, *Paterson*			X	X	X
James and the Giant Peach, *Dahl*	X	X	X		
Julie of the Wolves, *George*		X	X	X	X
Kidnapped, *Stevenson*		X	X	X	X
The Lion, the Witch and the Wardrobe, *Lewis*		X	X		
Little House on the Prairie, *Wilder*	X	X	X	X	X
The Little Prince, *De Saint-Exupery*	X	X			
Little Women, *Alcott*			X	X	X
Midnight Fox, *Byars*	X	X	X		
Mrs. Frisby and the Rats of Nimh, *O'Brien*		X	X	X	
My Side of the Mountain, *George*	X	X	X	X	X
Old Yeller, *Gipson*		X	X	X	X
One-Eyed Cat, *Fox*			X		
The Outsiders, *Hinton*				X	X
The Owl's Song, *Hale*			X	X	X
Paddle-to-the-Sea, *Holling*		X	X		
Peter Pan, *Barrie*		X	X	X	X

TITLES GRADES:	4	5	6	7	8
The Phantom Tollbooth, *Juster*		X	X		
Queenie Peavy, *Burch*		X	X		
Ramona and Her Father, *Cleary*	X	X			
The Red Pony, *Steinbeck*				X	X
Robinson Crusoe, *Defoe*		X	X	X	X
Roll of Thunder, Hear My Cry, *Taylor*		X	X		
Sign of the Beaver, *Speare*	X	X	X		
Sing Down the Moon, *O'Dell*			X	X	X
Stuart Little, *White*	X	X	X		
Summer of My German Soldier, *Green*		X	X		
Summer of the Swans, *Byars*		X	X		
Tuck Everlasting, *Babbitt*		X	X	X	X
The Velveteen Rabbit, *Williams*	X				
Walkabout, *Marshall*			X	X	X
Where the Lilies Bloom, *Cleaver*		X	X	X	X
Where the Red Fern Grows, *Rawls*		X	X		
The Wind in the Willows, *Grahame*	X	X	X		
The Witch of Blackbird Pond, *Speare*		X	X		
A Wrinkle in Time, *L'Engle*		X	X		
The Yearling, *Rawlings*			X	X	X
Zeely, *Hamilton*	X	X	X		
Zia, *O'Dell*	X	X	X		

CHAPTER 8

SPELLING

Research shows that there is no direct correlation between intelligence and spelling. Some gifted students have tremendous vocabularies and can spell virtually anything; others have great difficulty spelling even the simplest of words. Just because a student reads well doesn't mean he or she can automatically spell well. So it is best to have three options available to individuals in the gifted group when it comes to spelling.

If the student:

1. Isn't a very good speller, use the same speller the rest of the class uses.

2. Is a competent speller but has difficulty spelling the irregular vocabulary words from the reading, assign a speller a year or two above the student's grade.

3. Is an excellent speller with a good vocabulary, use vocabulary words from the literature book.

These options will comfortably accommodate every student in the gifted group.

The words each student learns will vary, but the generic spelling assignments listed in this chapter will work, no matter how diverse the various word lists may be. Daily assignments will be written on the board and will be due on Friday.

The spelling activities included develop all six thinking levels of Bloom's Taxonomy. It must be noted that these activities can be used by students in the regular class who are not necessarily gifted but who are talented in spelling.

A list of ten to fifteen words is recommended for the spelling test, but adjustments for student ability can be made. When giving the spelling test on Friday, the teacher will give all of the words to the entire class. This provides an opportunity for regular students to take the gifted words for extra credit if they wish, or, when the regular spelling list is finished, they can simply sit quietly, reviewing their own words until the entire test is complete. Spelling can remain an entire group activity this way, and will not require a disproportionate amount of teacher preparation time.

SPELLING ACTIVITIES

Knowledge:

- Recall words on an orally given test.

Comprehension:

- Understand the definition of the word by writing the dictionary definition.

Application:

- Use the word correctly in separate sentences.
- Make a crossword puzzle of the words and their definitions.
- Illustrate the meaning of the word.

Analysis:

- Add prefixes and suffixes to each word. Explain how they change the meaning.
- Add or subtract letters from the word to create a new word.
    Example: stop – s = top
                   stop + o = stoop
- Categorize spelling words in some way (i.e., alphabetically, by parts of speech, number of letters, configuration, etc.).

Synthesis:

- Invent own words and definitions. Write the pronunciation of the word and its part of speech (noun, verb, adjective, etc.), then use the word in a story.
- Translate the words into another language either real or imaginary, and use them in a story.
- Make up own definitions of real words, explain and illustrate them.
- Write a story using all spelling words correctly in context.

Evaluation:

- Critique the sentences or paragraphs in the literature book, substituting other words for the spelling words, and explaining why the changes are better.
- Use Latin and Greek roots to evaluate the origins of the words.
- Predict which words are most commonly used and why.
- Recommend different pronunciations for words and justify them.

For the rare gifted student who has extraordinary spelling and vocabulary skills, the synthesis activity of inventing his or her own words is suggested. By making up words, writing definitions, and using the words in a story, a gifted student is functioning comfortably at his or her level and applying every spelling skill there is. A typical assignment could be to create five adjectives, five verbs, and five nouns. These students are few and far between, but this activity allows their minds to run free into higher realms unencumbered.

A SAMPLE WEEK OF ASSIGNMENTS

n overview of the whole class's activities is provided below. A sample week of assignments for the gifted group follows.

MONDAY	TUESDAY	WEDNESDAY	THURSDAY	FRIDAY
Opening	Opening	Opening	Opening	Opening
Read Aloud/Inst	Read Aloud/Discuss	Read Aloud/Discuss	Read Aloud/Discuss	Read Aloud/Discuss
Newspaper Article "President Visits China." List important points on board.	Chaps. 1–2 Mrs. Frisby and the Rats of NIMH	Chaps. 3–4 Mrs. Frisby and the Rats of NIMH	Chaps. 5–6 Mrs. Frisby and the Rats of NIMH	Chaps. 7–8 Mrs. Frisby and the Rats of NIMH
Writing Assignment	Journal	Journal	Journal	Journal
Summarize article using important points listed on board.	Write about a time someone was sick in your family.	When the tractor started, what do you think Mr. Fitzgibbon was thinking? What was Mrs. Frisby thinking?	Draw and write a cartoon of what you would say to the owl if you were Mrs. Frisby.	Chain how the story would change if Jeremy had not taken Mrs. Frisby to the owl.
				Spelling Test
				Lit. Activities
(Low Group if needed)	Low Rdg. Grp. Middle Rdg. Grp. High Rdg. Grp.	Low Rdg. Grp. Middle Rdg. Grp. High Rdg. Grp.	Low Rdg. Grp. Middle Rdg. Grp. High Rdg. Grp.	– Puppet Show of story events – Map Fitzgibbon farm – Collage shiny things Jeremy likes
GIFTED GROUP*				GIFTED GROUP*

* Close-up of daily activities on subsequent pages.

MONDAY

READING

Before: Come to the group with ideas about why a person would have a secret name and not tell it to anyone.

Read: Chapter 4, *Island of the Blue Dolphins*. A secret name is revealed in this chapter. See what happens as a result.

Journal: Choose your own secret name, record it, and decorate your journal by illustrating why you chose it.

WORKBOOK

Pages 15 and 17 (drawing conclusions).
Do all problems. Then write three passages from which others can draw a conclusion.

SPELLING

abalone	decreed	ponder	sandpit	stout
abound	forlorn	portioned	solemn	surged

TUESDAY

READING

Before: List what your reactions would be if one of your family members were killed.

Read: Chapter 5, *Island of the Blue Dolphins*. Find out Karana's reaction when someone in her family is killed.

Journal: List how your reactions might be similar to and different from Karana's.

WORKBOOK

Pages 28 – 30 (adjectives), odd numbers. List ten objects in the room and adjectives to describe each of them.

SPELLING

Write a paragraph using five of your spelling words properly.

WEDNESDAY

READING

Before: Write how you would feel if you were part of the tribe and saw another ship.

Read: Chapter 6, *Island of the Blue Dolphins*. See what reactions seeing a new ship brings.

Journal: Chain what you think will happen when Karana leaves her island.

WORKBOOK

Pages 41 and 51 (punctuation), even numbers. Use at least two of each of the punctuation marks correctly in your spelling story.

SPELLING

Write a story about Karana in *Island of the Blue Dolphins* using the five spelling words you did not use yesterday. (Remember, use two of each of the punctuation marks correctly.)

THURSDAY

READING

Before: Draw five items you would pack if you were moving.

Read: Chapter 7, *Island of the Blue Dolphins*. Read to see what Karana packs.

Journal: Compare the items Karana packed with those you packed by listing similarities and differences.

WORKBOOK

Pages 48 and 74 (fact/opinion), all problems. Write five factual statements and five that are opinion.

SPELLING

Categorize your spelling words by part of speech and list them alphabetically.

FRIDAY

READING

Before: Think about all the decisions Karana made in chapters 4–7 in *Island of the Blue Dolphins*. Be prepared to discuss them.

LITERATURE ACTIVITIES

Choose one to complete with a friend:

- PUPPET SHOW—Put together a puppet show about the events in chapters 4–7 from Ramo and Karana's points of view.

- MODEL/MAP—Construct a model or map of the island, and label where the events in the story have taken place so far; include a key to the map.

- DIARY—Write a diary from Karana's point of view, and tape-record it, speaking with feeling and adding sound effects as they are needed.

BIBLIOGRAPHY

Anderson, Gordon S. *A Whole Approach to Reading*. United Press of America, 1984

Anderson, Richard C., et. al. *Becoming a Nation of Readers: The Report of the Commission on Reading*. U.S. Department of Education, 1984.

Bloom, Benjamin, ed. *Taxonomy of Educational Objectives, Handbook I: The Cognitive Domain*. McKay, 1956.

Brown, Linda Nayes. *Think Book*. Incentive Publications, Inc., 1990.

Clark, Barbara. *Growing Up Gifted*. Merrill, 1979.

Cochran, Judith. *Insights to Literature, Middle Grades*. Incentive Publications, Inc., 1990.

Cochran, Judith. *Incorporating Literature into the Basal Reading Program*. Incentive Publications, Inc., 1991.

Forte, Imogene and Schurr, Sandra. *Science Mind Stretchers*. Incentive Publications, 1987.

Frender, Gloria. *Learning to Learn*. Incentive Publications, Inc., 1990.

Heimberger, Mary J. *Teaching Gifted and Talented in the Elementary Classroom*. National Education Assoc., 1980.

Hirsch, E. D. *Cultural Literacy*. Vintage, 1988.

Renzulli, Joseph S. *The Enrichment Triad Model: A Guide for the Gifted and Talented*. Creative Learning Press, 1977.

Treffinger, Donald. *Encouraging Creative Learning for the Gifted and Talented*, National/State Leadership Institute on Gifted and Talented, 1980.

Trelease, Jim. *The Read Aloud Book*. Penguin, 1989.

Zattel. Jeffrey J. *The Education of Gifted and Talented Children from a Federal Perspective*. U.S. Educational Resource Information Center, 1980.